IT'S TIME TO EAT A DESERT QUANDONG

It's Time to Eat a Desert Quandong

Walter the Educator

SKB

Silent King Books
A WhichHead Entertainment Imprint

Disclaimer

This book is a literary work; the story is not about specific persons, locations, situations, and/or circumstances unless mentioned in a historical context. Any resemblance to real persons, locations, situations, and/or circumstances is coincidental. This book is for entertainment and informational purposes only. The author and publisher offer this information without warranties expressed or implied. No matter the grounds, neither the author nor the publisher will be accountable for any losses, injuries, or other damages caused by the reader's use of this book. The use of this book acknowledges an understanding and acceptance of this disclaimer.

DESERT QUANDONG

"Time to Eat a Desert Quandong!"

It's Time to Eat a

Desert

Quandong

It's time to eat, what's this I see?

A bright desert fruit waiting for me!

Round and red, with a shiny skin,

A desert quandong, let's begin!

From the outback land where the sun shines bright,

This special fruit grows with all its might.

Under hot skies, in sandy ground,

That's where this desert gem is found.

Oh, quandong, so bright and sweet,

A desert fruit that's fun to eat!

Red and round, with a taste so new,

Quandong, I'm ready for you!

I pick you up, so smooth and bold,

A treasure in the desert's gold.

Not too big and not too small,

It's Time to Eat a

Desert

Quandong

You fit in my hand, and I won't let you fall!

I take a bite, what's that taste?

\

A mix of tart, not a bit to waste!

You're tangy and fresh, a little sour,

But full of desert's secret power!

Oh, quandong, so bright and sweet,

A desert fruit that's fun to eat!

Red and round, with a taste so new,

Quandong, I'm ready for you!

Inside your skin, what do I find?

A little seed that's left behind!

Shiny and smooth, round and neat,

It's like a stone, but oh so sweet!

You're not just food, you're more than a snack,

People use your seed for a craft attack!

They carve and polish, they make things bright,

Your seed shines like a star at night.

But for now, it's time to munch,

A quandong snack is the perfect lunch!

It's Time to Eat a

Desert Quandong

In pies or jams, you're just so good,

A tasty treat from the desert wood!

Oh, quandong, so bright and sweet,

A desert fruit that's fun to eat!

Red and round, with a taste so new,

Quandong, I'm ready for you!

ABOUT THE CREATOR

Walter the Educator is one of the
pseudonyms for Walter Anderson.
Formally educated in Chemistry,
Business, and Education, he is an
educator, an author, a diverse
entrepreneur, and he is the son
of a disabled war veteran.
"Walter the Educator" shares his
time between educating and creating.
He holds interests and owns several
creative projects that entertain,
enlighten, enhance, and educate,
hoping to inspire and motivate you.
Follow, find new works, and stay
up to date with Walter the Educator™

at WaltertheEducator.com

Milton Keynes UK
Ingram Content Group UK Ltd.
UKHW021937281024
450365UK00018B/1146

9 798330 463664